YOUR TIME, YOUR GOALS AND YOUR IDENTITY

Agency Growth Need Not Be Difficult

Learn To:

Simplify Your Agency's Growth

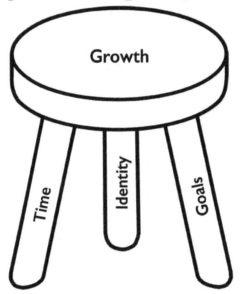

Agency Growth and Three Legged Stools Are Similar
Neither Work Well Without All Three Legs

BILL LYNCH

outskirts press

Your Time, Your Goals and Your Identity
All Rights Reserved.
Copyright © 2018 Bill Lynch
v5.0

The opinions expressed in this manuscript are solely the opinions of the author and do not represent the opinions or thoughts of the publisher. The author has represented and warranted full ownership and/or legal right to publish all the materials in this book.

This book may not be reproduced, transmitted, or stored in whole or in part by any means, including graphic, electronic, or mechanical without the express written consent of the publisher except in the case of brief quotations embodied in critical articles and reviews.

Outskirts Press, Inc.
http://www.outskirtspress.com

Paperback ISBN: 978-1-4787-4802-1

Cover Photo © 2018 www.gettyimages.com. All rights reserved - used with permission.

Outskirts Press and the "OP" logo are trademarks belonging to Outskirts Press, Inc.

PRINTED IN THE UNITED STATES OF AMERICA

Table of Contents

Introduction v

First Leg . . . Time—Your Most Valuable Asset 1
Control My Day 3
The Control My Day Work Sheet 5
The Control My Day Challenge 6
My Friends the Frogs 9
Miscellaneous Time Ideas 11

Second Leg . . . Goals—Be Successful on Purpose 15
Last Year's Results 19
Gut-Check Questions To Ask Yourself 21
My Bob Gould Story 23
Let's Get Started 25
(Current Month) Agency Production Goals 28
Is Change Really Necessary? 29
Your Closing Ratio 30
Some Suggestions To Improve Your Closing Ratio 31
My Thoughts On New Business Commissions 34
Motivate Yourself 37

Third Leg . . . Identity—What Makes You Unique? 39

#1. My Story and Promises 40
- Call Us Anytime 44
- On a Scale of One to Ten 45
- Have a Conversation with Your Clients 47

#2. Action Plans Make Your Agency Different 48
- Template for Action Plans 50
- Action Plans 51
- Example: Converting Quotes to
  Longtime Clients' Action Plan 54
- Example: My Agency's
  Life Insurance Action Plan 58

#3. Financial Risk Review Can Make You Different 62
- Financial Risk Review 65
- Financial risks we all face: 65
- The Why and How of a Consistent
  Financial Risk Review 66
- Call Us Anytime 71
- Death Is a Financial Risk 72

#4. Staffing Can Make You Different 75
- So You Want an Irreplaceable CSR 81
- Ideas on How to Be an Irreplaceable CSR 84
- Standards/Behaviors Inherent For All Positions 88

#5. Miscellaneous . . . Smart Activities 90
- Xdates 93

Introduction

For forty years, I was a Farmers Insurance Agency owner. I started my career in 1974. If I'm honest, I was not an overnight success. For the first six or seven years, I was my own worst enemy. Even though I was working hard, my bad attitude stopped me from taking responsibility for my poor results. My poor results were never my fault. Noncompetitive rates, underwriters that were unreasonable, and really crazy company decisions were always the cause of my problems (sound familiar?). When I had a problem, which I often did, that problem could ruin my whole day, and many times, my whole week.

Thankfully, I had help from a great district manager who finally convinced me it was time to look at myself in a mirror and take responsibility for my poor results. Also, he taught me to let go of problems I had no control over. Slowly but surely, my improved attitude allowed me to become successful. I share this with you because I am in a unique position to share not only my success but also my failure because I was not an overnight success.

When I retired, my current district manager asked me to share my agency experiences, with the hope current agents would benefit. So, for the last four-plus years, I have been meeting with District 22 agents. I've done my best to share what I believe helped me overcome my shortcomings.

I made copies of the forms and documents I used as an agent. I gave a great deal of thought to what I did and why I did it. I put many of those thoughts on paper and e-mailed and/or used them in face-to-face meetings. As you can imagine, I accumulated stacks of paper dealing with many different subjects.

So Now What?

What follows is my attempt to organize my thoughts into some logical order. Years ago, I was in a class where the instructor used a drawing of a three-legged stool to illustrate the three main points of his presentation. I thought it was effective. So I found a drawing of a three-legged stool and will use it to organize the subject of agency growth into three different but important topics. Each leg or topic is necessary if we are to achieve agency growth.

Leg One . . .   Time—Nothing can happen if you can't control time.
Leg Two . . .   Goals—Know what you want and how to get it.
Leg Three . . . Identity—Who are you, and what do you do? Be unique.

Most of the information I share with agents is not original. I am the beneficiary of many agents and instructors who took the time to share their knowledge. I hope you find this information useful, and if you do, please pass it on to others.

Thank you,

Bill Lynch

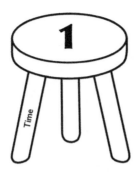

First Leg...Time—
Your Most Valuable Asset

One of the most important lessons I learned as an agency owner was how important the ability to manage time was to my success. I had been told many times that time management was important, and I always paid lip service to the idea of time management. But truth be known, it took awhile before I fully understood just how important the ability to control my time would prove to be. I worked hard every day, but seldom completed the activities necessary to make my agency a success. I learned the hard way; just knowing time management was important was not enough. I had to develop the *discipline* to make time control my number one priority.

What follows are ideas I used in my agency and use today to coach agents about how important time is to the success of their agency. I know from experience if you can control your day, your agency's success will be simplified.

How do you manage your time?

Don't Miss:

Control My Day

The Control My Day Work Sheet

The Control My Day Challenge

My Friends the Frogs

Miscellaneous Time Ideas

Control My Day

The number one event that finally helped me develop the discipline to control my day happened at a company conference in Ashland, Oregon. At that meeting, an accountant from Arizona shared what he did to control his day. He literally changed my life!

But first some background . . . Looking back, I'm surprised I even attended that meeting. Back at the office, I was buried in paperwork. I was busy but not productive. I bounced from one busy task to another. My life was not fun. I know I would never have been successful if I hadn't made his plan my own.

His plan was simple if I could only commit to it.

Only three *must-do* activities:

#1. Take time today to plan for a productive tomorrow.

#2. Do today only the tasks and phone calls that are most productive. The real moneymakers.

#3. Keep everything else off your desk. No distractions.

Although the basic plan was simple, it was not easy at first. But once I got control of my day, there was no way I was going give up that control. Having control gave me real power to manage my time and Simplify My Agency's Growth.

How would YOUR life change if you really had control of your time?

The Control My Day Work Sheet

Date _____

Appointments		Calls To Make Today	Things To Do Today
Time	Who	Who	What
____	_____	_____	_____
____	_____	_____	_____
____	_____	_____	_____
____	_____	_____	_____
____	_____	_____	_____
____	_____	_____	_____
____	_____	_____	_____
____	_____	_____	_____
____	_____	_____	_____
____	_____	_____	_____
____	_____	_____	_____
____	_____	_____	_____
____	_____	_____	_____
____	_____	_____	_____

I will take a moment today to make sure my tomorrow is productive. I will list the things that I want to do, the calls I want to make, and, of course, the appointments I will keep. I will know what I want to accomplish tomorrow before I go home tonight. This is how I will be in control of my day. And because I control my day, I will be more productive. I can make decisions about time based on what I want to accomplish. I love having control of my day!

The Control My Day Challenge

If we all have only twenty-four hours each day, why does it seem like some people can accomplish so much more than the rest of us? How is it possible they easily do all the things we never seem to have the time to do? The only possible answer is that they do a better job managing the same time we all have. I believe our ability to manage time is directly related to how successful we can be. If that's true, and I believe it is, our number one priority must be to do a better job controlling our day. If you take "The Control My Day Challenge," it will help you manage your time and change the way you look at yourself and change forever how you manage your agency.

Who: Agents who want to be more productive.

How: Complete The Control My Day Work Sheet for fourteen consecutive days. The work sheet for tomorrow *must be completed before you go home tonight. This is critical to the success of this challenge.*

What will happen: If you make a commitment to do all the required steps of The Control My Day Challenge, you will change how you look at yourself and your agency. In fourteen days, this will be a habit you won't want to break. *You will be more productive!*

Appointments: Before you go home today, list all the appointments you have scheduled for tomorrow. The things you can accomplish and the calls you can make tomorrow will depend on how many appointments you have scheduled. Listing your appointments will help you be realistic about what you can accomplish.

Things to do and calls to make: Your desk and computer task file are full of things to do and calls to make. What you have to do is sort through the mess and find the really important things to do and calls to make. You are looking for *only* the items that will make you productive and *have* to be done tomorrow. The moneymaker things. At first, this will be difficult because you have so many items to do and calls to make. With experience, you will learn that not everything has to be done tomorrow. Only the very most important things to do and calls to make should be on your list. Remember, no system is perfect, so you will have to stay flexible.

Items that don't make the list: Items that don't make the list have to be delegated to staff or set aside for the day they have to be done or round filed. The Control My Day process will make you a better delegator. You will learn to ask your clients questions like: "When do you need this information?" You will learn that not everything that hits your desk today has to be done today. You will make decisions about time based on what you want to accomplish today. I put the things to do and the calls to make that didn't make my list for today in an alphabetical pending file. I attached a Post-it note with a date on each item. This was the date I felt was the day each item had to be done. With computers, you may want to use a task file.

The Result: At first, trying to juggle these activities will seem complicated. But with your determination to control your day, you will find the process liberating. You will discover that when you control your day, you actually have more time for your family. You will find the longer you use The Control My Day process, the better you will feel about yourself and your agency.

 # My Friends the Frogs

About twenty-five years ago, I attended a sales conference and was lucky enough to hear a very good speaker from Texas. I could tell he was from Texas by his Southern drawl and the entertaining way he could tell a story.

The story he told that day had a big impact on me and the way I ran my agency. He started his talk by asking us something that I thought was a silly question. He asked, "If you had to . . . absolutely *had to* swallow a frog, would you want to swallow a small frog or a big frog?" We all laughed and looked at each other because we weren't quite sure where he was going with this goofy question. He then said, "You all have frogs sitting on your desks back at your offices. Many of the frogs are small frogs because they have just been put there since you have been gone. Some others are large because you left them there before you left. The only thing I know for sure is they are all growing and will continue to grow until you take care of them." Of course, he wasn't talking about real frogs. He was talking about the problems we leave undone. The longer we ignore the problem, the bigger the problem gets. So . . . would you rather swallow a small frog or swallow a big frog?

I thought the comparison between frogs and problems was clever and made notes so I could share it with my staff. Later that same day, I found myself in the gift shop. I never realized people actually collected small ceramic animals like cows, pigs, and you guessed it, frogs. I bought one for myself and each member of my staff. My idea was that we'd each keep this small frog on our desks to remind ourselves that we didn't want this frog/problem to grow because we'd rather swallow a small frog than swallow a big frog.

As you may have guessed, my staff thought I had lost my marbles, but because I wrote their paychecks, they humored me. Soon, we were referring to problems as frogs and that we had better solve the problem now while they were small problems because no one wanted to swallow a big frog.

Soon, friends, family, and clients thought I was a frog collector and brought me more frogs. Some of you that visited my office may have noticed my "frog collection."

How do you handle YOUR frogs?

 # Miscellaneous Time Ideas

Are You Like Me?

Does your work expand to fill whatever time you have to complete your work, and strangely, contract when you have less time to complete the same work? Mine does! Here's an example: If I have ten tasks to complete by noon, it will take me the full morning to complete those tasks by noon. But if I have to complete those same tasks by eleven, somehow, I manage to get them done by eleven. Crazy! Conclusion: If I'm not careful and pay attention to my time, I can waste time and not even realize it.

How do you monitor how long you and your staff spend doing everyday tasks? How could we do better?

How About This?

My wife Kathy would occasionally ask me what I'd done today. I'd think about it for a minute and admit I really had no idea. But what I did know was I was buried; I didn't even have time to grab lunch. One day, it finally hit me. I was always busy. I didn't have time to attend important meetings. I didn't have time to keep up with industry and company changes. And sadly, I even missed some of my kids' games. But as busy as I was, I was not very productive. My achievements did not reflect how hard I was working.

Something had to change. I started to pay attention to my everyday activities. I started to divide my activities "B" for busywork and "P" for productive work. Once I was paying attention to what I was doing, I was amazed how often I could bundle my busywork or delegate my busywork to my CSR. When I didn't have a CSR, paying attention to what I was doing convinced me I needed a CSR. Paying attention to my busy and productive work helped me focus on what was truly important. Being aware of what you do every hour of every day is the key to being productive . . . not just busy.

How can I change to be more productive, not just busy?

Frank Bettger . . .

Frank Bettger, in his famous book, *How I Raised Myself From Failure To Success In Selling* (which I recommend), says we should work smarter not harder. He says if we spend more time planning what we do, we won't have to work as hard getting it done. Frank also believed we should all join the six a.m. club. I took his advice and was amazed at how much I could do before my staff arrived and the phones started to ring. Think of all the activities you could accomplish if you started earlier . . . Work *on* your business not just *in* your business; catch up on all that busywork. Just think how great you will feel when you aren't too busy to do the fun and productive work.

How much time do I spend planning what I will and won't do?

What could I accomplish if I had started earlier?

Second Leg ... Goals—
Be Successful on Purpose

In my opinion, Agency Growth is virtually impossible if you don't set goals. Setting goals gives your agency a road map for success. You may never achieve all your goals, but that's OK. The important part of goal setting is the *goal setting process.* Sure, results are important, but thinking through what it is you want and what you are willing to do to get what you want is the reason we go through the goal setting *process.*

The *goal setting process* forces you to look objectively at your current situation. Where are you now? What did you accomplish this year, this month, this week? Because you take the time to review where you are, you can realistically set goals that make sense for your agency. The *goal setting process* encourages you to choose only the goals that excite you and your staff. Once you know what you want, you must take the time to work on the "How-To." What does your agency need to do to accomplish your goals? If you skip this important step, your goals may never be more than wishful thinking.

Now that you know what you want and how to get it, you must find a way to make yourself accountable. Sharing my goals with my staff, my wife, and sometimes my DM helped me stay accountable. Another reason to include your staff is if you want them to buy into what it is you want to accomplish, they must know what that is. Knowing your goals makes them a part of your team. Last but not least, you have to stay focused. I broke my goals down to monthly goals and checked my progress every week. I had a staff meeting every Monday morning. At that meeting, we discussed our monthly goals and measured our results for the last week. I believe this helped us stay focused on what still needed to be done to accomplish our monthly goals. Also, staying focused was another way to control my time.

Here are the five steps needed to complete the goal setting process:

1. Know *where you've been and where you are now.*
2. Pick goals that *excite you and your staff.*
3. Know what your *agency needs to do* to achieve your goals.
4. Share your goals to *stay accountable.*
5. Track your results weekly to *stay focused.*

I set goals for everything. PIF goals, income goals, production goals, and activity goals. Goals helped me stay motivated. *Goals helped me push myself when I really didn't want to work. Goals helped me improve how I did what I did.* I know I would not have been as successful if I had not embraced the *goal setting process.*

In the last couple of months of each year, I spent a great deal of time making plans for the next year. I thought it was important to have expectations of what I wanted my agency to accomplish. I never accomplished all of my goals, but I'm certain my agency was better because I went through this process.

I was once told that before you could know where you were going, you had to know where you had been. With that in mind, I made certain I had a clear picture of how my agency looked today. I've attached a work sheet (Last Year's Results) that might help you see your agency as it is today. Any research you may have to do will be time well spent.

I've included some gut-check questions you can use to go beyond just the numbers. It's important you be honest with yourself, so you can get a clear picture of where you are today.

If you are to accomplish anything important, and I believe your goals are important, you have to believe in yourself. For many years, I didn't really believe in myself. That changed when I met with Bob Gould. Please see the attached *Bob Gould Story*.

What comes next are some thoughts, work sheets, and actual goals I used in my agency and use now when I meet with agents.

Be sure not to miss:

* An example of forms to record last year's results

* Gut-check questions to ask yourself

* My Bob Gould story helped me believe in myself

* A form to record results weekly

* Is change really necessary?

* Your closing ratio is important

* Commission goals

* Motivate yourself

What kind of goals get YOU excited?

How will you stay accountable and focused?

The work sheets that follow may not fit your agency but will work as an example of the kind of information you need.

Last Year's Results

***New Policies

	Auto	Fire	Life	Commercial	Specialty	Totals
Jan						
Feb						
Mar						
Apr						
May						
Jun						
Jul						
Aug						
Sep						
Oct						
Nov						
Dec						

***Where Did Policies Come From?

	Auto	Fire	Life	Commercial	Specialty	Totals
Customers						
Cross Sell						
Win Backs						
Producers						
Leads						
Solicited						
Other						

SECOND LEG ... GOALS—BE SUCCESSFUL ON PURPOSE

Last Year's Results

***More Numbers

Monthly Folio Total PIF FFRs Life Appointments XDates

Jan _____

Feb _____

Mar _____

Apr _____

May _____

Jun _____

Jul _____

Aug _____

Sep _____

Oct _____

Nov _____

Dec _____

Totals _____

These are last year's numbers. Study them. Are they better or worse than you expected? Either way, do you know why? Look for areas that you know you can improve.

Gut-Check Questions To Ask Yourself

Now is the time for some tough questions.

*** Was my glass half-full _____ or half-empty ____ last year?

*** Did I control my day ___ or did my day control me? ___

*** How much time on Monday did I spend to make sure Tuesday was productive? _____

*** On a typical day, I worked _____ hours a day. Was that too many hours ___ too few hours ___ or about right? ___

*** On a typical day, was I productive? Yes ___ No ___

*** Did I take responsibility for my results? Yes ___ No __

*** How many employees did I have? ___ Too many __ Too few __

*** Did I set a good example for my employees? Yes ___ No ___

*** Was I a Top-Ten Producer for any line of business? Yes _ No _

*** Did I take the time to stay informed of changes in my company and industry? Yes ___ No ___

*** What did I read that would improve my sales skills? _____

*** Overall, when I look at my agency, am I happy with my results? Yes ___ No ___

If deep down you know you can do better, you want to do better, then you need to plan to take advantage of the opportunities the new year will bring.

 ## My Bob Gould Story

I tell you this story now because I truly believe most of us are capable of much more than we accomplish. I think that the only thing that slows our progress is our lack of belief in what we can accomplish. I know this from personal experience.

Many years ago, I was, at best, an average agent. I was never a top producer and was frustrated that I was unable to grow my agency the way that it would provide my family the lifestyle I felt they deserved. Across the state, in La Grande, Oregon, agent Bob Gould was everything I thought I wasn't. Bob was my hero! Bob won all the production awards, went to President Council every year, and best of all, was a really nice guy. I also think he was responsible for the concept of offense-defense to help grow your agency. I truly believed Bob was in a different league, and that I could never achieve what he so easily seemed to accomplish.

Nick Watson, another frustrated agent, and I decided we needed to talk to Bob. I called Bob, and he gladly agreed to meet with us. Nick and I drove to La Grande, spent the night, and we were at Bob's office first thing the next morning. Bob spent the whole day with us, bought us lunch, and answered all of our questions. We left about three that afternoon because we had a long drive home. I don't remember all that Bob shared with us that day. But about three-quarters of the way home, we realized that Bob hadn't actually told us the most important lesson we learned that day. We learned that Bob, although successful, was not that much different than Nick or I. He really was not that much smarter. But what he had that we didn't was a deep belief that if he worked hard, he would be successful. Nick and I agreed that if Bob could do it, there was no reason why we couldn't do it. That trip to La Grande completely changed the way I looked at myself.

Bob ended up moving to Colorado Springs and became a district manager (go figure), and, sure enough, he was successful. One of my greatest joys in this business came a few years later. Nick and I both went to Presidents Council, and guess who was there as a district manager. You guessed it. Bob Gould. We bought him a drink and thanked again and again for his help. I don't think I'll ever forget the lesson I learned that day in La Grande: *If you truly believe you can, and are willing to work hard, you can accomplish almost anything.*

Who is YOUR Bob Gould? How did he help you?

If you don't have a Bob Gould, find one!

 ## Let's Get Started

Now that you have a clear picture of your agency, and you *truly believe* you can be successful, it's time to make your goals for next year.

Try to find three, no more than five, goals that even if only partially achieved, would make your year a success. This is your chance to make **your** wish list. Your chance to decide what **you** want your agency to accomplish this year. Only choose goals that get **you and your staff excited**. Normally, your company's and your goals will be similar, but push come to shove, focus on the goals that get **you** excited.

At this point, your next year's goals are nothing more than just a wish list. If this is all you were to do, your chance of success would be minimal. So how do you make a wish list achievable goals?

For each of your goals, you need a "How-To" work sheet that will act as a guide to how you hope to accomplish each goal.

The "How-To" for each of your goals should be a list of activities that, if accomplished, would lead to the achievement of your goals. The activities for each goal are reminders of the activities you must do to achieve your goal.

The "How-To" work sheets for each of your goals change wishful thinking to real possibilities. Without the "How-To" work sheets, your goals can never be more than dreams you have little chance of accomplishing.

The hard part is to find the activities that, if done, will achieve your goals. Once you know the activities you need to do, you must be committed to getting them done.

Most of you will need help if you are to achieve your goals. You must share your vision of what your agency can be with your staff. Show them your goals and "How-To" work sheets. Help them buy into what your agency can accomplish. With their help, you can make your goals possible. Without them... Well, good luck.

If you have your list of three to five goals (wishful thinking) and the "How-To" work sheets (makes goals possible), you are well on your way to achieving your goals. But you all know that business goals, like New Year's resolutions, can be easily forgotten after just a few days or weeks. You need a way to keep yourselves focused.

One way to stay focused is to add a "Monthly Agency Production" form to your monthly sales record book. You can keep track of the policies you write in the sales record book and stay focused on the "Monthly Agency Production Form." (Page 28)

See the attached Monthly Production Form and note there are three sections to this form.

#1. Top of the form: Write in the current month and dates for weekly accountability. We had a weekly staff meeting every Monday morning . . . So if the first Monday was the 7th, the first space would be the 7th, second space was the 14th, then the 21st, and then the 28th. The last space was totals. At our meetings, we could discuss if we were meeting our goals on a weekly basis. It was very effective and kept staff involved.

#2. The left side of the form . . . Goals for the month. How many of this, how many of that. I filled this part as an example. You must use your own weekly goals and numbers. Remember your annual goals.

#3. The bottom left of the form: Where did the policies I sold come from? See the example. Again, you can keep track weekly.

This form helped us stay accountable and focused. It got my staff involved in what we were trying to accomplish.

Another way I tried to keep my staff involved was to make sure they knew how important our goals were to our agency's success. They knew if we weren't willing to change, our success might not happen. Please see the attached "Is Change Really Necessary?" I used this form whenever we discussed our goals.

I hope the information in "Setting Goals" is helpful. Again, I think your agency will be better if you take the time to go through this process.

.

(Current Month) Agency Production Goals

Stay Focused   1st Week, 2nd Week, 3rd Week, 4th Week . . . Totals

Choose your goals   _____   _____   _____   _____   _____

__ **Total Policies**

__ **Life Policies**

__ **Commercial**

__ **FFS Sales**

__ **Referrals**

__ **FFRs**

__ **Appointments**

Where did my policies originate?

Customers

Solicited

Referrals

Cross-Sells

Win Backs

Other

 # Is Change Really Necessary?

Somebody pretty smart once said, "It is foolish to expect different results if we continue to do the same things."

So, yes, I have to change!

I have to take charge of my day and get serious about what it is that I will do, and maybe just as important . . . What I won't do to achieve our goals.

I have to be willing to *let go* of the day-to-day operation of my agency to my staff. They are good. I know they are good. I have to let go.

I have to empower my staff to become sales focused. I must insist that they provide excellent customer service while they cross-sell our services.

I must do whatever it takes to be face-to-face with our clients.

We have no control over our results, only our activities.

# Your Closing Ratio

*** How To Find Your Closing Ratio

When you divide the number of sales you make by the number of quotes you gave to make those sales, you get your closing ratio. For example: If today you made three sales as a result of the ten quotes you gave, your closing ratio is thirty percent.

*** Why Is Your Closing Ratio Important?

Your closing ratio is your report card. It tells you how well you are doing . . . or not. Improving your closing ratio gives you the motivation to make the changes you need to make to grow your agency. Improving your closing ratio forces you to think through the how and why you do what you do. Improving your closing ratio is one of the ways salespeople get better. So, finding ways to improve your closing ratio is extremely important, because ultimately, your goal is to be more productive . . . not just busier.

Some Suggestions To Improve Your Closing Ratio

*** The Right Time

Knowing when to give your presentation or quote can improve your closing ratio. Giving your quote when there is a sense of urgency to make a decision is the best time. Giving your quote when you are comparing your current price with his new price makes sense. So be patient; only give your quote when your chance to get a good hearing is the best.

*** The Best Person

Knowing who should give your presentation or quote can be a huge way to improve your closing ratio. In most agencies, the right person to quote your best prospects is the agency owner. The agency owner is the most invested in his business. That's not to say that a good CSR or producer can't give quotes; they can and should. But for the prospects you target as the prospects you really want to build your agency around, why gamble that an employee can deliver your presentation with the same enthusiasm you can? So for those special prospects, improve your chance of success by giving those quotes yourself. Let your employees quote the prospects you feel are less valuable . . . The cold calls . . . The price-only prospects . . .

*** The Right Presentation

If you want to improve your closing ratio constantly, look for ways to improve your presentation. What makes your agency different? What can your prospects expect from your agency? What promises does your agency make and keep? If your enthusiasm for your agency is contagious enough, you will get your prospects to buy into your vision for their security, and if you do, your closing ratio can't help but improve. Your presentation is your opportunity to show your prospects you offer more than price. Your presentation can convince your prospects there is a difference between price and real cost, and you know what it is.

*** Educate Your Prospects

When you take the time to educate your prospects, you can drastically improve your closing ratio. How many of your prospects know what 100/300/50 means? How many of your prospects know the value of an Umbrella? When you take the time to educate your prospects, your value grows, and price is less important. Time spent educating your prospects and clients about the insurance they buy is never wasted.

*** Keep Accurate Records

Keeping records in itself won't improve your closing ratio, but it is essential to know what works and what doesn't. I started by keeping track of how many times I dialed the phone on what day and at what time. Keeping track of how many people answered helped me determine the best time I should make calls. Keeping track of how prospects responded to my message helped me improve my message. Keeping track of the quotes I gave and the sales I made helped me develop a closing ratio. Once I had my closing ratio, I could work to improve it. If I hadn't kept track of my activities, I would have no way of knowing what worked and what didn't. So, yes, keeping accurate records is essential to improving your closing ratio.

How do you keep track of YOUR closing ratio?

My Thoughts On New Business Commissions

When I was a new agent, the only income I could count on was new business commissions. I hadn't been an agent long enough that I could depend on renewal commissions to feed my family. I knew it would take a few years before I would make more money on renewals than I did new business commissions. So, it was important that I could find a way to earn enough new business commissions to stay in business. This worked for me, and I suggest you try it.

The first thing you need to know is how much new business commission you need. Most companies offer a subsidy, but you may not want to count on your subsidy to stay in business. You may consider your subsidy your safety net. Once you know the amount of new business commission you need, you can start planning how you can earn it. This process will work even if you are not a new agent. It works for anyone that has a new business income goal.

Once you know your income goal, you have to divide that number by the different lines of business you sell. What percentage of the total will be auto, fire, or life new business commissions? Now that you know the income goal for each line of business, you need to know what your average commission is for each line of business. It's important that you use your numbers. Don't use company averages. To find your average commission, divide your total commission per line of business by the number of policies per line of business you have sold. You now have the average commission for each policy in each line of business.

Now you need to find how many policies you need to sell to reach your new business commission goal in each line of business. Divide the average commission for each line of business into the income goal for each line of business, and you have the number of policies you need to sell.

Now that you know how many policies you need to sell, you need to know your closing ratio. Your closing ratio is the number of quotes/presentations you need to give to sell one policy. Divide your total number of sales by the total number of quotes/presentations you needed to make those sales, and you have your closing ratio. Your closing ratio tells you how many quotes you need to give to get the sales you need to achieve your new business goals.

Now The Fun Part

As you go through this process, it becomes obvious how important accurate records are to your success. Now that you know how many quotes/presentations you need to give, and how many sales you need to make, you can now start improving your results by playing the *what-if* game.

What if you gave more quotes/presentations than you needed to meet your new business commission goals? How would *that* improve your bottom line?

What if you could improve how you delivered your quotes and presentations? *What if* you stopped relying on price to sell your policies? *What if* you sold your agency story and promises? How would *that* improve your bottom line?

What if you were more selective? *What if* you stopped wasting time on prospects that don't know the difference between price and cost? Do you think your closing ratio and bottom line results would be better?

What if the policies you sold generated more commission? Full coverage, not just liability, permanent not term. How would *that* improve your bottom line?

What would your bottom line look like if you could not only give more quotes, but quoted better prospects, gave better presentations, and sold bigger policies?

You may agree the fun part of being an agent is keeping and studying your records and finding ways to improve how you can reach your goals. This process will motivate you to give more quotes, find better ways to present your quotes/presentations, look for better prospects, and increase the value of each sale.

I hope this helps.

Basic Goal Setting . . . Start with a goal and work backward . . .

Motivate Yourself

If you are looking for a way to get motivated, why not get motivated by competing against yourself? Each month, pick the lines of business you want to improve and work to best your last month's production numbers. No matter how big or how small the numbers, focus on beating last month's numbers. Some months, these numbers may appear to be unbeatable, but still try. Your effort will help you reach higher levels of achievement than you might otherwise achieve.

Activities To Beat Last Month's Results

#1. Pick goals that excite you. Examples might be: Total number of policies, GWP for personal lines, commercial or life.

#2. Share your goals with your staff, a mentor, or your spouse. Sharing goals makes you accountable.

#3. Find and use the "how-to" achieve your goals. What activities will your agency need to do to achieve your goals?

#4. Track your progress at least weekly. This will also help you control your time.

#5. Note your end-of-month results and resolve to beat these results next month, no matter how big or small.

#6. Results You now have an effective way to get motivated by beating yourself. Your results will continue to improve as long as you focus on your monthly goals. Look at your results last month. What could you do to improve? If you focus on your goals and what needs to be done, you can't help but succeed.

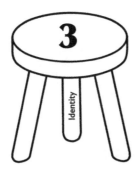

Third Leg ... Identity—
What Makes You Unique?

The first two legs of Agency Growth are no-brainers. Who could argue time control and goal setting are not critical to agency growth? But what about that third leg? What's the one thing along with time control and goal setting that is necessary for an agent to develop agency growth? In my opinion, an agent must establish a unique identity. His identity must make his agency appear to be different from his competitors. Your identity is not just who you are, but also why your agency is the best choice for your clients. What do you do that your competition doesn't? When I say identity is the third leg of agency growth, I mean identity in the broadest sense. Who you are, what do you believe, what you do, how you do it, are all part of your unique identity. An identity that hopefully stands out from your competition. What follows are ideas I think made my agency unique.

#1. My Story and Promises

#2. Action Plans

#3. Financial Risk Reviews

#4. Staffing

#5. Misc. Smart Activities Xdates

# #1. My Story and Promises

Years ago, I read *The E-Myth Revisited* by Michael Gerber. The "E" stood for entrepreneur. This is a great book about managing business. At the end of the book, I noticed an invitation to call the Gerber Institute if we thought we could use some help with our business. Long story short, I called and was assigned to a Gerber Institute business consultant named Tom who worked out of his office in San Diego, Ca. Every two weeks, we had a two-hour phone appointment. At this appointment, we discussed ideas that, if implemented, would improve my business. Tom knew nothing about insurance, so these meetings were strictly business management meetings. I hope to share here some of the more valuable bits of information I learned at these meetings.

Tom asked many questions about my business. Questions that made me really think about my business. Why do I want to own my own business? What will my business look like in five years? Why should anyone choose my business to protect their family? How am I different from the agent down the street? What do I offer that he doesn't? He helped me look at my business not as a Farmers Insurance Agency but as the Bill Lynch Agency. Once he convinced me that what I was really selling and what my clients were really buying was not Farmers Insurance but the Bill Lynch Insurance Agency, it was easier to find ways to make the Bill Lynch Agency different. We spent a great deal of time discovering what it was that made us different. But knowing we were different was not enough. I now had to learn how to communicate our difference to our prospects and clients. Merely being different was not enough.

Tom then said something I'll never forget. He said, "Don't be afraid to tell your story. Don't be afraid to brag a little. If you don't, who will? How will your clients know you're different if you don't tell them?" He encouraged me to take my difference and make it a story. A short story that, if delivered with passion and sincerity, communicated to our clients why they should choose the Bill Lynch Agency to protect their families.

Tom then told me if I was truly going to be different, I would need more than just a story. He asked me what I thought were the biggest complaints the average client had with our industry. He assured me if I could correctly answer that question, I'd have all the information I needed to make sincere promises to the people I wanted as clients. The two almost universal complaints I observed were: 1. I never hear from my agent. He sold me this policy, and I haven't heard from him since. 2. They never call me back. I leave message after message, and it takes them forever to return my call.

I started to use my stories and promises whenever I tried to convince prospects I had more than price to offer. Could I convince a prospect if I was $300 higher? Not very often. Could I convince a prospect if I was $300 lower? Almost always. But what about the prospect I saw the most often? The prospect that was paying about the same price as our price? I'm sure my story, given with passion and my promises delivered with sincerity, have been able to convince my share of new clients that the Bill Lynch Agency delivered the most value for their premium dollar.

I've changed my story many times to fit different prospects, but my promises have stayed the same from day one, delivered with sincerity and passion like this . . .

When you choose the Bill Lynch Agency, we make you two very important promises that we do our very best to keep.

Promise #1 . . . We will take whatever time is necessary to make sure you have all the information you need to make good insurance decisions. This promise includes the opportunity to meet face-to-face at least once each year to review all of your insurance policies.

They know we are serious because we show them that we have prescheduled their appointment. As and Bs in January, Cs and Ds in February . . . and so on. See the attached. (Page 44)

Promise #2 . . . We will return all phone calls, answer all questions, handle all problems within twenty-four hours. If you call us in the a.m., we will return your call that same p.m. Your p.m. calls will be returned no later than the next a.m. We may not have all your answers, but you will know we have not forgotten you.

How do you convince your prospects to change if you aren't the cheapest?

What promises do you make and keep? How are you different?

What follows is a collection of stories and promises I've used over the years. I've also included some papers I've written to share with agents I meet.

Call Us Anytime . . . A form I used to let clients know I was serious about keeping promise #1.

Our Story and Promises . . .

On a Scale of One to Ten . . . An idea of when to use your story and promises.

Have a Conversation . . . I used when I got my securities license.

Call Us Anytime

But note, we have set aside a time to keep our promise to review your insurance

Appointment Schedule

January	A B
February	C D
March	E F
April	G H
May	I J
June	K L
July	M N
August	O P
September	Q R
October	S T
November	U V
December	W X Y Z

Mark Your Calendars!

# On a Scale of One to Ten

As an agent, I always looked for opportunities to tell my story and to give my promises. I believed if I could passionately tell my story and sincerely give my promises, my prospects were less likely to judge my agency on price alone. But often I struggled to find the best time to give my story and promises. Recently, I heard what I consider an excellent way to introduce your story and promises. I know if you play with the words and make what you say your own, your clients will be less concerned about your price and much more likely to "buy into" what your agency has to offer.

So here goes:

Whenever you or your producer make or take a call from your prospect, you or your producer say, "On a scale of one to ten, how would you rate your current agent or your agent's customer service?" Wait for an answer. If his answer is a nine or ten, say, "That's really good; you must be happy with your agent." Listen to what he says. If he's happy, I'd say something like, "I was once told if it wasn't broke, don't fix it." Thank him for his time and move on. Even if you could beat his price, the chances of your getting the business are slim because he has a relationship with his agent.

However, if his answer is anything but a nine or a ten, you have a great opportunity to win his business. The lower the score, the better. Encourage your prospect to vent. You may find your prospect doesn't even know his agent. Ask your prospect why his current agent deserves only whatever number he gives him. Be sympathetic.

You or your producer can introduce your agency. Say something like, let me tell you about my agency or the Bill Lynch Agency. Then give your story and deliver your promises with all the passion and sincerity you can muster. You are trying to contrast his number whatever with your great number ten agency. The bigger the difference, the less price will make in his decision. We know if we give him enough good reasons to change, price won't be the deciding factor.

Will this work with everyone every time? Of course not. But I believe it will work often enough to improve your closing ratio.

Good luck,

Bill

Why I think this approach works:

You're asking for a number to rate his agent, not if he wants a quote. No mention of price. You're comparing agencies—not cost.

 # Have a Conversation with Your Clients

. . . Our goal/purpose/mission is to help you understand the *sometimes complicated* policies you need to protect what you have.

Insurance! Auto, Home, Life Insurance. Explain to your client how these policies can be complicated.

. . . Also, we want to help you make sense of the *truly complicated* products you need to grow what you have.

Traditional and Roth IRAs, Annuities, Mutual Funds. For sure, these products confuse most of your clients. Give examples . . .

Simply put, we want to help you protect and grow what you have.

Remember . . . Your best clients and prospects will appreciate you are offering something tangible that most of them need.

#2. Action Plans Make Your Agency Different

After my consultant convinced me how important my story and promises would be to my identity, he showed me how I could manage my agency as a real business. Tom explained that successful businesses used systems for almost everything they did. Important and even not so important work was never left to chance. I told him this all seemed complicated, but he assured me it wasn't. All I needed to do was learn how an action plan could solve almost any problem or frustration my agency encountered.

Tom showed me the Action Plan Template (see attached), and he was right; it was not complicated. It was actually simple. Tom then warned me that simple didn't mean easy. Again, Tom was right. Although simple in concept, the action plan required we think through our problems and find perfect solutions and the actions needed to attain those perfect solutions. Simple, yes, but not always that easy.

What do you do to solve agency problems?

Does your agency have a written "how we do it here"?

What follows:

*** **Template For Action Plans**

*** **The Action Plan Template**

*** **Step-By-Step Instructions To Complete An Action Plan**

*** *Example:* **New Business Action Plan**

*** *Example:* **Converting Quotes To Long Clients Action Plan**

Template for Action Plans

_____ Action Plan   Date _____

I. Problem or Frustration . . .

II. Ideal Solution to Problem or Frustration
    The Result Expected . . .

III. Benchmarks. The Step-by-Step Process to
     Achieve the Ideal Solution . . .

IV. The Standards and/or Behaviors Necessary
    to Achieve Results. The Who, What, Where,
    When, and How . . .

Action Plans

A well thought out action plan can help you manage your agency many different ways.

1. Action plans can help you and your staff solve almost any problem or frustration your agency encounters. The action plan process helps you think through your problems/frustrations to find the ideal solution.

2. If you have an action plan for each task your agency needs to accomplish, you will have created a standard way of doing things. *The way we do it here.* Action plans make training new employees easier. A new employee needs only to look at your action plans to see how your agency handles each task.

3. Action plans can be the *how-to* for the goals you set. It's one thing to have a goal, but it's quite another to know how you are going to accomplish that goal. Action plans can be the *how-to*.

See the attached Action Plan Template (Page 50)

Name your action plan. Agencies that get serious about action plans have plans for virtually every task their agency wants to accomplish. McDonald's is an example of a business that uses action plans to make sure each task is done the same way every time. That's one way they can assure a hamburger tastes the same anywhere you go.

Date. You may want to review your action plans. Things change, and you may need to update how you *do it here*. The date will make sure you are using the most current plan.

I. *Problem/frustration or task* . . . Is there a problem that needs to be solved? A frustration to be fixed? A task that needs to be systematized? It can be as trivial as no coffee in the morning or to the important things like, why don't we have at least five life appointments a week? Whatever the problem/frustration, a well thought out action plan will help you and your staff solve that problem or frustration and help you develop a standard way to do all the tasks that your agency needs to accomplish.

II. Ideal solution to the problem or frustration. The result expected. If you had a magic wand and you could wave it, what would the ideal solution look like? You may have to stop and think, but think big. What you are looking for is the perfect solution to the problem or frustration; i.e., the best way to handle each task.

III. Benchmarks . . . The step-by-step process to achieve the ideal solution. Benchmarks are the meat of your action plan. The how do you get that perfect solution. Finding the right benchmarks to give you the perfect solution is the most important part of your action plan. Each benchmark is an action. If you complete all the actions, you will get that perfect solution. The action plan process will help you and your staff think through your problems or frustrations. Some action plans may have only two or three benchmarks; other more complicated action plans may have many benchmarks. The goal is once all your benchmarks are completed, you should have the ideal solution. Remember, benchmarks are not written in stone. Your staff may have suggestions that will improve the likelihood that if done will lead to the ideal solution. The action plan process will help you think about what you are doing and if what you are doing is the most effective way of doing it. Finding the right benchmarks to solve your problems will not be easy, but the reward is worth the effort.

IV. *The standards and/or behaviors necessary to achieve results. The who, what, where, when, and how . . .*

Unlike benchmarks, the standards and/or behaviors are the touchy-feely part of the action plan. They may not directly lead to the ideal solution, but without them, the ideal solution may be more difficult to attain. Standard and/or behaviors use words like . . . Smile . . . Empathize . . . Always . . . Never . . . Think About. If you fail to include standards and/or behaviors in your action plan, you may be missing the opportunity to train your staff. Sometimes it's not just what we do, but the way we do things that make the difference between success and failure.

I hope action plans work for you as well as they did for me.

Do YOU think Action Plans could work for you?

Example: Converting Quotes to Longtime Clients' Action Plan

Problem/Frustration

Our quote conversion to policy rate is low. Many of the conversions we do get don't turn into longtime customers. Too many times, we end up with a single line of business. We get frustrated with our poor results, and because of our frustration, we don't quote as often as we should. We blame rates for our lack of success.

Ideal Solution

We now convert __% of the quotes we give into longtime clients. We now quote households, not single-line policies. We don't waste time on shoppers. We now concentrate on prospects that recognize the value of insurance. We now find gaps in coverage and fill them. Since we have changed our attitude, we realize we have more to offer than price. *Giving quotes is almost fun.*

Benchmarks

A. Recognize, as agents, we have never been happy with the rate we charged for insurance. Even in the "good old days," we complained that we were not competitive. I know. I was there!

B. Buy into Frank Bettger's "Don't Be Afraid To Fail." Frank tells us to let the law of averages work for us. It can change our attitude about repetitive tasks.

C. Gather as much information about our prospect as we can. We can never know too much about our prospect.

D. Make account selling the way we do business. Let our prospect know we expect to quote and insure his autos, home, and life insurance.

E. Use a checklist to make certain we offer our prospects the best rates possible. Double-check our numbers.

Before we give our numbers . . .

F. Tell him our story. Give him our promises. Show our prospect; we are different than any other insurance agency. Sell our agency. Be passionate. Get excited and make him want to do business with our agency. (See a template for our story and the promises I used for years at the end of this action plan.)

G. Ask for an appointment. If we've made a connection, ask to meet. We can be more passionate in person than over the phone. Remember, 100 percent of the people we don't ask won't meet with us. But if we ask, who knows? If he can't meet with us, he will still appreciate that we asked. We may have been the only agency that wanted to meet with him. Perhaps his own agent doesn't want to talk to him. Asking makes us different.

H. Don't assume our prospect wants the lowest price. Price may be important if price is all we give him to make his decision. Remember the four currencies . . . Price . . . Time . . . Feeling safe . . . Feeling special . . . Surely, we can make our prospects feel safe and feel special. If we do, we will have a client for life, or at least for a very long time.

I. Expect that prospects that pay about the same or a little more or less than our quote to change to our agency. If we go in with the mind-set that we offer more than price and truly believe he will be better off with our agency, then why shouldn't he change? Really, a no-brainer!

J. Give our quote. If we can't meet in person, give our quote over the phone. Be confident and assume he will choose your agency.

K. Keep accurate records of our results. Study our results. Know what works and what doesn't work. Continue to improve our presentation. Know the dollar value of each call, quote, and conversion.

Standards and/or Behaviors

A. Treat the quote process as an event. Recognize giving a quote is an important way to grow our agency and the first impression our new client will have of our agency.

B. *Everybody in our agency will use this action plan every time. NO EXCEPTION!* This is how we do it here.

C. Always smile and be passionate, enthusiastic, and excited.

Outline for Our Story and the Promises I Gave for Years

Our story should be a short statement about what our agency is about. What we believe. How we treat our clients. What makes us different. Our mission statement. It's important that our story and the promises we make are delivered with passion. Our story and promises must get us excited. Our prospects must be able to feel our excitement.

Promise #1. We will take whatever time is necessary to make sure you have all the information you need to make good insurance decisions . . . That promise includes the *opportunity to meet face-to-face once a year to review all of your insurance policies . . .*

Promise #2. We will return all phone calls promptly . . . If you call us in the morning, we will return your call that afternoon. If you call us in the afternoon, we will return your call the next morning. We may not have all the answers that soon, but we'll call to let you know we haven't forgotten you.

# Example: My Agency's Life Insurance Action Plan

Frustration/Problem

My agency doesn't offer or sell life insurance. We don't seem to buy into the idea that life insurance is the most important coverage we offer. When we do present life insurance to our clients, it is often presented as a product, not as a solution to a need. Because we too often sell product, it is difficult to get staff involved. As a result, our agency life numbers are embarrassing.

Ideal Solution

My agency buys into the importance of life insurance, and because we do, we offer our clients the coverage they need to protect their families. Selling life insurance is no longer just a job to satisfy a need to meet company requirements but a mission to fulfill a promise we make to our clients. Because we made this attitude adjustment, life insurance policies are sold, relationships are being built, and our agency is a success.

So what does success look like? My agency sells _____ to _____ policies a month. We sell solutions to a need, not just policies. Need selling has increased the average face amount, improved our lapse ratios, and helped us retain our clients. Because I now "buy into" need selling, my staff follows. Since my staff has the most contact with our clients, their "buy in" is essential. My staff responds much better to need selling than they do to product selling. I'm proud to say life insurance is now a major focus for our agency.

Benchmarks

A. We must make an attitude adjustment.

1. Show "Life Happens" videos at all staff and training meetings. These videos will demonstrate need.

2. Make life insurance a topic of discussion at staff meetings. Take time to discuss the need for life insurance.

B. Simplify the concept of life insurance to the basics. Client dies, insurance company pays. Staff doesn't really need to know how IUL, VUL, and FFUL policies work. Come to think about it, neither do many of our clients. All they need to know is that they do work. Illustrations can help *us* understand the policy, but rarely do illustrations help your staff and clients. Be careful with them.

C. We must sell Need . . . Mortgage Insurance, Income Insurance, Education Insurance, and Legacy Insurance. Remember, clients don't want life insurance; they want what life insurance does. So we must find out what they want and give it to them.

D. We will set goals and keep accurate records. Goals and records make us better. How can we fix what we don't know is broken?

E. We must make the life bonus a big deal. We will know how the life bonus works and set goals to earn the life bonus. Include staff in the payoff.

F. Learn and practice openers: Do you or don't you ever worry that . . . Are you or aren't you concerned that . . . What's the one thing you want to leave your family?

G. Have a life insurance story that we can deliver with passion and sincerity. Maybe as simple as: Here are my three reasons I buy and continue to pay for life insurance . . . guaranteed home, education, and income. Have a go-to need and a go-to policy.

H. Offer larger policies. We can always go down, and more times than not, your clients will buy what we offer.

I. Become a student of our business. If a new policy is introduced, make sure we study the illustrations so we can present the policy in a way your client will understand.

J. Develop a consistent and ongoing policy review program. There is no better time to present solutions to needs than during a policy review.

K. Misc. . . . Don't forget to follow up. Be persistent. Become competitive, even if it's with yourself. Learn to ask good questions.

Standards/Behaviors

A. Be sincere . . . Use the test: Would I sell this to my brother/sister?

B. Remember, protection always comes first.

C. Always remember: God forbid, someday we may have to deliver a check; make sure we won't have regrets about the size of that check.

D. Today's no can change to a yes when "life happens." Be persistent!

E. Have fun!

 # #3. Financial Risk Review Can Make You Different

Policy reviews always made sense to me. I felt we owed our clients the opportunity to review their coverage. Wasn't that what we did when we sold the policy? Didn't we make sure our new clients had the right coverage? Didn't we promise always to be there? Well, to me, the policy review was my way to be there.

For the first few years, I reviewed my clients' policies whatever way my company thought was best. And that was OK. It wasn't until I attended a Life Underwriters meeting at the Inn at the Mountain that I got really excited about policy reviews. That meeting was a real game-changer for me. Instead of doing policy reviews because I thought I should, now I did them because I knew I was making a real difference.

The guest speaker at that meeting was a State Farm agent from Florida, and his story changed the way I did policy reviews. Because of hurricanes, State Farm had put a moratorium on new businesses. The only new business he could write was new business for current clients. He had to meet with his clients if he wanted to write new business. So he did what most of us would have done. He called his clients, convinced them they needed a policy review, hoping he could either add policies or at least increase coverage for his current clients. Many of his clients weren't interested in increasing coverage, and he, instead, ended up adding discounts and raising deductibles. The end result was little or no income was earned doing policy reviews. He knew he had to find a more profitable way to do policy reviews. What he did next changed everything.

He decided he no longer wanted to discuss individual policies. He found whenever he focused on this car policy or that car policy, this home policy or that boat policy, the conversation often became a price-only conversation. Because he didn't want to talk about individual policies, he decided to take the policy out of the policy review. He decided to change the name of his meeting to a Financial Risk Review. Financial risk is what he wanted to discuss, so, he chose five financial risks we all face:

Disability . . . What happens if I can't work?

Health . . . What happens if I get sick?

Liability . . . What happens if I'm sued?

Death . . . What happens if I die too soon?
What happens if I live too long?

Property . . . What happens if my property is destroyed?

Please see the attached Financial Risk Review form (Page 65)

The next part was brilliant. He described his job for this review. *My job is to bring to your attention the financial risks that face your family.* The next part is even smarter. He described the client's job for this review. *Your job is to determine how you want to handle these risks, because you do have choices.* He gave the client choices. *You can retain the risk, you can eliminate the risk, you can reduce the risk, or you can the transfer risk.* He then gave the client examples of each choice. The client could retain the financial risk his mean, nasty dog posed. He could take full financial responsibility for his dog. He could eliminate the risk by getting rid of the dog. Or he could reduce the risk by tying the dog up. When he discussed transferring risk, the question of to whom came up.

He explained we transfer risk all the time. We transfer risk to the government (Social Security). We transfer risk to our employer (health and disability insurance). And, of course, we transfer risk to our insurance companies. What he said next made him a true adviser, not just a salesperson. He said, *"It's not my job to convince you to transfer your financial risk to my insurance company. My job, as I see it, is to bring to your attention the financial risk you and your family face. And if you want, give you the cost to transfer that risk to us, your insurance company."*

He discussed each financial risk as one risk. For example, liability was liability for all types of liability: auto, home, boat. Loss of property was loss of property for all types of property from all causes of loss.

I've used this form hundreds of times. The financial risk review form makes doing policy reviews fun for me and informative for my clients. I've attached a paper titled, "The Why and How of a Consistent Financial Risk Review Program." If you are as serious as I was about policy reviews, you will find this paper helpful.

P.S. Over the years, I've used the concept of transfer or retain whenever I didn't want to appear to be *that* salesman. Let *them* choose. *Generally, the cost of transfer was less than the risk of retain.*

Financial Risk Review

* My job is to bring to your attention the financial risks that face your family.

* Your job is to determine how you want to handle those risks. You do have choices about how you handle risk.

1. Retain   **2. Eliminate**   **3. Reduce**   **4. Transfer**

* Implement or maintain your plan.

Financial risks we all face:

Disability: What happens when I can't work?

Health: What happens if I'm sick?

Liability: What happens if I'm sued?

Death: What if I die too soon or live too long?

Property: What happens if I lose my property?

# The Why and How of a Consistent Financial Risk Review

After forty years as a Farmers Insurance agency owner, I am convinced that the single most important service I offered my clients was the policy review. I called my review The Financial Risk Review. What you call it is not important. What's important is that you have an ongoing, consistent way to meet and review your client's coverage. When I first started doing reviews, I had no idea how important they would become to my agency's success. I will try to give you the reasons I maintained a consistent Financial Risk Review program with the hope you will benefit by starting your own consistent program. I will also share a few ideas on how to get started and attach the Financial Risk Review form I used hundreds of times. (Page 65)

My Reasons

** I promised our prospects and clients the opportunity to meet with me face-to-face each year to review all of their policies. I did my best to **keep my promise**.

** A consistent Financial Risk Review program made us a **proactive** agency. This program gave us a reason to reach out to our clients consistently.

** I am certain that our Financial Risk Review program helped us build **relationships,** which, in turn, improved my **retention ratio.**

** I am certain our consistent Financial Risk Review program improved our agency's **penetration** into our client's household. Although the Financial Risk Review was not designed to be a sales meeting, it was almost impossible not to **cross-sell and increase the limits** on our clients' coverage.

** Most, if not all, the **life insurance** I sold originated in the Financial Risk Review. (Page 65)

** One last reason a consistent policy review was important to our agency is when I reviewed my clients' coverage, I could **educate** them on how important a good insurance program was to the financial security of their family.

Let's Get Started

Here is an outline of what I feel is important to a consistent, ongoing Financial Risk Review program. Please note, I've attached the Financial Risk Review form I used every time I did a Financial Risk Review.

** Commit to making an ongoing, consistent Financial Risk Review program the way you do business. This is not a one-time program, rather a year in, year out way to service clients. You should do Financial Risk Reviews every day.

** Start soon: Use the Financial Risk Review to sell your agency to your prospects. Include it in your promise to your prospects/clients.

** Show your prospects/clients your Financial Risk Review schedule. Make them believe you are serious by showing them you have prescheduled their Financial Risk Review appointment. As and Bs in January. Cs and Ds in February, and so on.

** The Financial Risk Review has to be simple and easy to understand. You are offering a service, not page after page of policy descriptions that do nothing but confuse your clients. Your Financial Risk Reviews should rarely include anything more than the Financial Risk Review form. Now, that's not to say you won't get them the information they request; but less is better when it comes to paper.

** See the attached form. Use the phrases, "My job . . . Your job." Explain your job is to point out the financial risks his family faces. His job is to determine how he wants to handle those financial risks. Make him aware he has choices. Choices #1 and #4 are the ones to emphasize. Retain means he accepts the risk and does nothing. Transfer means just that. He can transfer risk to the government. Examples might be Social Security and Medicare. He can transfer risk to his employer. Examples might be health and disability insurance. His employer may even provide limited life insurance, but is it enough? And, of course, he can transfer risk to you, his insurance company. Make sure he understands it's not your job to convince him to transfer all his risk to you. *Your job is to make sure he knows what risk he is retaining, and if he wants to transfer that risk, what it will cost.* You are no longer a salesperson! Your job is to bring to his attention financial risk and let him decide how he wants to handle it. He does have four choices.

** Explain to your clients "the good news and the bad news." For example, the good news for health is that most of your clients have transferred that risk to their employer. The good news for death, dying too soon, may be that their employer provides some life insurance; the bad news is that it may not be enough. The good news for liability is that they may have transferred $100/$300/$50 to you, but the bad news is they are responsible if that is not enough coverage. You will sell a lot of umbrellas with this discussion. Good news, bad news, and the transfer—retain concepts can be used for all of your clients' financial risks. Use your imagination and have fun with it.

** You may have noticed I don't talk about individual policies. Liability is liability for everything: auto, home, boat, or whatever type of liability risk your clients face. Loss of property is all types of property: auto, home, boats . . . whatever property your client owns. How the property is destroyed makes no difference. Death is both living too long and dying too soon. Use the terms *transfer* and *retain* instead of *covered* and *not covered*.

** Never target renewal dates for Financial Risk Reviews. If you have a Financial Risk Review on a renewal, it is completely coincidental. Your experience tells you reviews on renewal dates turn into price discussions. You don't want to talk price; you want to talk coverage. You want to make sure your client is comfortable with the risk he retains.

** As you may have guessed, the Financial Risk review was most effective for me with a face-to-face meeting with my client. Do everything in your power to make sure you are face-to-face. Never set your own review appointments. It was too easy to be trapped into doing a phone review. You may be different, but I was never as effective on the phone as I was in person. Recognize your clients are busy and offer to work around their schedule. If not now, how about after the holidays or in the spring? Continue to set them up for future dates until they figure just maybe this must be important.

** I can't tell you how many times my clients thanked me for doing the Financial Risk Review. Many of them went through the same review more than once and still thanked me. I think the reason the Financial Risk Review was so well received was that most of my clients never thought their insurance was about the choice of transfer and retain. They never thought in terms of good news/bad news.

** Bottom Line An ongoing, consistent Financial Risk Review is the one program you *will never regret starting*. It is a win/win for both you and your client.

I hope this paper is helpful and encourages you to make the Financial Risk Review an important part of your agency. Please call if I can be of help . . .

Call Us Anytime

But note, we have set aside a time to keep our promise to review your insurance

Appointment Schedule

January	A B
February	C D
March	E F
April	G H
May	I J
June	K L
July	M N
August	O P
September	Q R
October	S T
November	U V
December	W X Y Z

Mark Your Calendars!

 # Death Is a Financial Risk

We Live too Long, or We Die too Soon

Most, if not all, of the life insurance I sold was the result of a Financial Risk Review. During a Financial Risk Review, I would explain to my client that my job was to bring to his attention all the financial risks that his family faced. His job was to decide how he wanted to handle those risks. I made sure he realized that he did have choices. I explained his choices were: he could retain the risk and accept responsibility, he could eliminate the risk, sell the car, he could reduce the risk and be careful, and, of course, he could transfer the risk. Transfer to whom? His employer, sometimes the government, and, naturally, insurance companies.

I made sure he understood that my job was *not* to get him to transfer his risk to me. My job was to make sure he *knew what risk he was retaining* and what it would cost if he chose to transfer that risk. I was no longer just the salesperson trying to sell more insurance. I was the person that made sure he understood what risk he was retaining and the person who showed him how he could transfer that risk, if he chose to do so.

Please see the attached "Financial Risk Review" form. This is the form I used hundreds of times whenever I did a policy review. I made a big deal of the choices he had to make to solve his financial risks problems. At each risk, we discussed his choices. Did he want to retain, eliminate, reduce, or transfer his risk? I pointed out that for most risks, there was good news and bad news. For example, when we discussed auto liability, the good news was he had already transferred to his insurance company $100,000 per person and $300,000 per accident to pay for injuries he caused. The bad news was that he retained or was responsible for any dollar amount above the coverage he had.

When I got to death as financial risk, I'd say something like… Death is a double-edged sword. We can live too long or die too soon. When we think about living too long, we think about retirement planning. With retirement planning, there is good news/bad news. The good news is you may have transferred some of this risk to your employer. Your employer may provide a pension or a 401(k). The bad news is it may not be enough, and you retain the risk of not having enough money to retire. At this point, it's easy to ask questions about what he has transferred. Does your employer provide a pension? Does your employer have a 401(k)? Does your employer match? What percentage of your income do you contribute? Do you have a Roth IRA? You may now have asked enough questions that he is concerned that he is retaining too much of the risk for living too long.

Now, I'd say something like: In my opinion, dying too soon is the most catastrophic financial risk we all face. Without proper planning, we have little hope of ever financially recovering from the death of a breadwinner. But again, there is good news/bad news. The good news is that you may have transferred some of the risk for dying too soon to your employer. Questions I'd ask: Does your employer provide life insurance? How much coverage does he provide? I was always amazed that many clients didn't know how much coverage they had at work. Have you transferred risk to other insurance companies? How much? The bad news: Don't you worry, or aren't you concerned that the coverage you now have won't be enough to keep your family in their home or provide enough income to maintain their standard of living? Maybe we should talk!

I'd go on and discuss loss of property as a financial risk. I continued to use the terms *transfer* and *retain* instead of *covered* and *not covered*. I wanted my clients to understand it was ultimately *their* choice how they handled *their* financial risk. I was no longer just a salesperson.

When I finished the property risk, I'd go back to each risk and review what we had discussed. This is when I'd try to get my clients to commit in a nonpushy way to transferring more risk to me. If I thought I'd hit a nerve discussing death as a financial risk, I'd show them my short "My Three Reasons" presentation or talk about "How Much Is Enough." I never tried to sell life insurance during a financial risk review because this was a service appointment, not a sales call. This is the review I promised them when we met. Depending on the situation, I'd schedule a second meeting.

From experience, I found the transfer and retain concept planted and watered a lot of seeds.

#4. Staffing Can Make You Different

When should you hire?

What comes first, the chicken or the egg? Whenever I thought about hiring my first employee or adding another employee, that's the question that always popped into my head. Should I hire an employee now, or should I wait till I have a bigger income? What happens if I can't afford an employee? Do I really need an employee? What happens if I hire the wrong person? All reasonable questions. In my own situation, I waited too long. I should have hired staff sooner. By the time I hired my first employee, I was doing way more busywork than productive moneymaking work. I didn't save money; I lost money by waiting.

I think if you are serious about adding an employee, you should understand how different your daily routine will be. Before you hire an employee, you do everything, but you know that, right? *That's* why you need an employee. But be careful; many agents are reluctant to give up or delegate the busywork they should no longer be doing. Remember, the only reason, and I mean the *only* reason, you have an employee is that your employee can now free up your time to do the productive moneymaking work you need to do to grow your agency. If you don't let go of the busywork, your new employee will become an expense, not an investment. That would be a shame and a waste of an employee.

What do you need?

OK, now you know you need an employee. Now what? I'm no expert. All I can do is share my collective experiences with employees. I learned the hard way I needed to know what I was looking for before I started the hiring process. I found that paying attention to the intangibles was huge. Is your prospective employee naturally friendly? Does he/she have a positive attitude? Does he/she seem ambitious? Do you think he/she could be a team player? Focus on the qualities you feel are important. I learned to pay attention to my gut, and if I had doubts, I probably should not hire.

Do I hire an experienced employee, or do I train them myself? Successful agents told me many times, experienced employees often come with baggage. Sure, they can do most of the transactions I needed. But many times, they came with bad habits or were set in their ways and found it difficult to do things my way. Often experienced employees found it difficult to "buy in" to my vision of what our agency could accomplish. On the other hand, they were already trained to do most of the transactions I needed. So the temptation to hire a trained CSR is strong but resist it. One more thought on the subject.

Earlier, I mentioned I had worked with a Gerber Institute business consultant named Tom who had a unique insight on employee experience. He not only did not think experience was valuable, he thought experience was a liability. He believed it was far better to hire someone with no experience but who was motivated to learn. Someone who was hungry for the opportunity to shine. Hire an overachiever, someone who will work hard to make the most of the skills she/he has. Tom thought this type of employee was more likely to "buy in" to agency goals and prove to everyone you didn't make a mistake when you hired her/him.

Job description or position contract?

The Gerber Institute had a unique way of looking at how employers should hold employees accountable. Tom thought job descriptions were a poor way to communicate to an employee what he was expected to do. I had to agree with him. Think about it . . . In most agencies with one employee, that employee's job description would be one word . . . *Everything.* As a result, both employers and employees are frustrated. The employee is frustrated because she does not know what she is responsible for. *I didn't know I was supposed to do that.* Sound familiar? The employer is frustrated because he does not get the result he expected.

Tom convinced me to replace my job descriptions with what he called position contracts. A job description is a list of activities done by an employee. *A position contract is a summary of the results to be achieved by each position in the agency, the work that position is accountable for, and a list of the standards by which results are to be measured.* Sounds complicated? Not really.

Example: A position contract for the position of claims manager for an agency. *Summary of results to be achieved by the claims manager.* What does a perfect result look like? Maybe . . . Our clients perceive their claims are handled fairly. They feel good about our agency. You could add a number of results that you might expect. *The work that the position of claims manager is accountable for.* This is all the work that needs to be done to achieve the results for the position of claims manager. Phone calls, follow-ups, contact the adjuster. Whatever needs to be done to achieve the perfect results. Another way of saying it is . . . Whatever it takes. *A list of standards by which results are evaluated for the position of claims manager.* The touchy-feely, the who, what, where, and how activities were completed for the position of claims manager.

Each employee in an agency may be responsible for more than one position. Both the employer and the employee sign the position contract, so there's is no confusion as to what is expected. This is not a job description; it is a contract between the agency and employee. The position contract provides each person with a sense of commitment and accountability. Position contracts will change how you look at employees and what they do for your agency.

Employee "buy in" difficultIt if not impossible to succeed without it.

OK, so now you have employees. Now what? Now the really important work begins. Now you have to convince your employees to "buy in" to your vision of what your agency wants to accomplish. Your employees must enthusiastically join the team. (Of course, this is easier if you hire wisely.) In my opinion, "buy in" is more important than all the transactions he/she will have to learn.

The One Minute Manager by Kenneth Blanchard and Spencer Johnson helped me encourage my employees to "buy in" to my agency more than anything I had ever read. Their simple but powerful message of positive reinforcement made training fun. They taught me to see and reward the positive and correct the negative in a nonpersonal way. If you want "buy in" from your staff, this book is a must-read.

What follows illustrates how I used "buy in" to grow my agency.

As I became more successful, I was asked to share ideas that helped my agency grow. This was impossible to do without talking about the huge contribution my staff made to my success. Often agents would remark how lucky they thought I was to have my Julie or Carol or whoever as an employee. Of course, I agreed. Then I'd ask questions about their employees. *Did your employees appear motivated when you hired them? Were they capable of knowing what you wanted?* If they answered yes to these types of questions, I'd suggest that maybe the problem was not their staff. Just maybe, the agents needed to reevaluate how they could get more "buy in" from their staff.

After I retired and started working with agents, I gave staffing a great deal of thought. My original question was . . . How do I get agency staff to "buy in" to their agent's vision? I soon realized that wasn't the real problem. In most cases, the agent was the problem. In most cases, it was the agent that had to change. In many cases, the agent didn't even have a vision. It was impossible to ask the staff to change if the agent didn't make some important changes. So I wrote two papers. One for the agent titled "So You Want An Irreplaceable CSR." This paper makes suggestions to help agents get the most from their staff.

The second paper for the CSR is titled "Ideas On How To Be An Irreplaceable CSR." I hope this paper helps your employee want to be irreplaceable.

I've attached both papers, and I hope you find them helpful. Also, I never had a formal employee manual (not sure that's smart), but I did use what we called. "Standards/Behaviors Inherent For All Positions." It's also attached.

Conclusion

Again, in my opinion, staffing is the most frustrating but also the most rewarding activity I did as an agency owner. My goal was to make their job not just a job. My hope was they felt like a part of a team. In most cases, I found I got what I gave. I'll end with this: I'm not naive enough to believe that on Monday morning, my staff was excited to get up and come to work. The best I could hope for was that if they had to get up and come to work on Monday morning, they were happy they were coming to work at the Bill Lynch Agency.

# So You Want an Irreplaceable CSR

All CSRs must be able to do all the activities any CSR does on a daily basis: Make car changes, take care of billing problems, and, of course, always be friendly to our clients. All these activities are important, but if this is all a CSR can do, they will never be irreplaceable, and since they are replaceable, most agents will be reluctant to increase their pay. Not a good situation for anyone. I call this type of CSR a *transactional CSR*. Does all the transactions an agency needs but very little else to help grow that agency.

Most transactional CSRs did not start that way. Most of us had high expectations of how our new CSR was going to help us grow our agency. But we were so concerned about the transactions being done correctly that most of the training concentrated on transactions, not relationships. Over time, we settled for the transactional CSR.

So how do we get our CSRs to do more than transactions? How do we get our CSRs to ask questions that lead to cross-selling and life appointments? How do we convince our CSRs that agency growth is the most important part of their job? And truly, agency growth is the *only* way we will be able to increase their pay. This will not be easy, but it is essential for agency growth.

I really don't think it's about more money. I know some agents who offer all kinds of incentives to convince CSRs to cross-sell and set appointments . . . with very little success.

If we are looking for long-term results, I think we have to change how we think about our agencies and realize if we don't change, it is unrealistic to expect our CSRs to change. We have to find a way to convince our CSRs to "buy in" to what we are trying to accomplish. We will have to become enthusiastic about our agencies and be willing to share that enthusiasm with our CSRs.

Our CSRs must know *we believe* in our "story and promises." They must know *we believe* our clients are better served by our agency than any other. We must show them *we believe* that price is only one of the four currencies, and that *we believe* the other currencies (saving time, feeling safe, and feeling special) can be more important than price alone. If you say customer service is important, be sure you give good service. Lead by example.

If you can be enthusiastic and convince them you are a believer, they *will* buy into what your agency wants to accomplish. And once they buy in, they *will* be irreplaceable. Congratulations. You did it!

Other Suggestions to Help Your Staff Buy In

Your staff knows nobody in your agency works harder than you. They know you wouldn't ask them to do anything you wouldn't do yourself.

Keep your staff informed. They should know where you are and when you will return at all times.

Share your annual, monthly, and weekly goals and results. If you want your staff to buy in, they need to feel they are an important part of your agency. Sorry, I meant *our* agency.

Have weekly and daily meetings. Weekly to go over results and share news and daily to make sure everybody is on the same page. Once every couple of months, have a lunch meeting and just talk to each other.

Make your staff feel like this not just a job. Make them feel important. Thank them often. Have fun.

Always look for the positive.

I hope this helps

Bill Lynch 503.407.7883 Bill@SimplifyAgencyGrowth.com

What are you doing now to convince your staff to "buy in"?

How do think an irreplaceable CSR could change your agency?

Are you afraid to make the changes necessary to have an irreplaceable CSR?

 # Ideas on How to Be an Irreplaceable CSR

If you are looking for *job security* . . . If you want more *job satisfaction* . . . If you want to make *more money* . . . All these things are possible if you can make yourself irreplaceable. To be irreplaceable, you will have to reevaluate what you think is important to your agency.

You may have been trained that you were expected to be friendly to the clients, make car and coverage changes, and help clients with their billing problems. Basically, to correctly do all the transactions your agency requires. And, of course, that's right. But if that's *all you can do,* you will *never* be irreplaceable.

An irreplaceable CSR must build relationships and ask the questions that lead to cross sales and life appointments. Your value to your agency is dependent on your ability and willingness to help grow your agency at the same time you are helping your clients. Think for a moment how irreplaceable and valuable you would be if you were responsible for three cross sales and four appointments each week.

No one has more contact with clients than the CSR. You are

the first to know when a home is bought or sold, when a job is gotten or lost. You have a real opportunity to help your clients and to grow your agency at the same time. All you have to do is pay attention to what your client is saying and ask questions. You could be responsible for a family being able to stay in their home if someone dies. You can make sure your client has the right coverage with the best agency.

When the phone rings, don't just think how fast you can do this transaction. Stop! Look at the client. What does he insure with your agency, and maybe more importantly, what *doesn't* he insure with your agency? Check out the comments. Is there something there you can talk about? If they went boating or camping last weekend, who insures the boat or camper? If a conversation about retirement comes up, has he saved enough? The breadwinner changed jobs. Does he still have life insurance? What about his retirement plan? Talk. Talk. Talk. Questions. Questions. Questions. You have a great opportunity to build relationships. And, oh, by the way, you are making your client feel special. Clients like to feel special, and if they do, they are less likely to leave your agency for price.

But you say, I'm not a salesperson. I don't like to sell insurance. I'm not good at selling. I don't want to be pushy. Well, good news . . . You don't have to sell or be pushy. All you have to do is like people, like to help people, be able to talk to people and ask questions. Your agent will take care of the rest.

From now on, your favorite words are: *You should talk to Bill. Bill is an expert on life insurance. Let's set up a time to meet.* Or, *What's the best time for Bill to call?*

You should talk to ____ You should talk to _____ You should talk to ____ Over and over. Try to say it five, ten times a day. Surely, *someone* will eventually want to talk to ____. And when they do, you will be irreplaceable!

Simple questions you can use to start a conversation:

Are you . . . or *Aren't you concerned that . . . ?*

Do you worry . . . or *Don't you ever worry that . . . ?*

Examples:

Auto/Home or I Have Progressive

. . . The insurance you bought online give you the protection you need when you need it the most?

I Have Life Insurance On The Job.

. . . Your family will have to move? . . . Your kids won't go to college?

Retirement Planning

. . . .You won't have enough money to retire?

These simple questions can help your clients think through the problems they may have with their present coverage. Problems they may not have even considered. These questions may also leave them open to your suggestion that: *You should talk to* ____

At first, you may find this process difficult. That's only because it's new. You will soon discover your clients actually appreciate your concern about their coverage. The End Result: You are now irreplaceable! You are now helping your agency grow! And most important, you are helping your clients be better protected!

I Hope This Helps . . .

Bill Lynch 503.407.7883 Bill@SimplifyAgencyGrowth.com

Standards/Behaviors Inherent For All Positions

Employees must maintain neat workstations. All employees are responsible for maintaining a neat and clean office.

Employees will dress professionally.

Work will be performed according to set procedures.

Customers and fellow employees will be greeted and treated in a friendly and professional manner.

Phone calls will be answered by the fourth ring courteously and professionally with a cheerful greeting, appropriately recognizing the time of day or holiday season.

Customer calls will end with a smile and a thank-you.

At 8:30 each morning, we will have a short office meeting to review yesterday and plan the upcoming day.

Each Monday morning at 8:30, we will meet for a weekly meeting to review the week and plan for the upcoming week.

An action plan will be written for each tactical work item.

All employees must be aware of our strategic objective and help the agency obtain marketing and service goals.

All employees must use the "Script" (story and promises) at every opportunity.

Employees will be tolerant of other employees.

We will be mindful that a team has a much better chance of success than any one individual.

All employees will be familiar with the Priority Grid. We will be mindful of what's *significant or not significant, and, of course, what's pressing and not pressing*. Then we will act accordingly.

All employees must know that the Bill Lynch Agency has an open door policy. Bill Lynch wants to help all employees achieve a profitable and meaningful career. With this in mind, it is important that you communicate your problems, suggestions, and concerns.

 # #5. Smart Activities

We know we can't always control our results, and we know we can't always guarantee our clients or prospects will buy. But what we can control is our activity. We can guarantee what it is we are willing to do to make positive results possible. Because our activity is so important, shouldn't we be certain our activity is smart activity?

What makes our activities smart activities?

1. Smart activities are activities done at the right time.

- ** Call, e-mail, or text only when your message is likely to be heard. Find the best time to communicate.

- ** Give your quote only if you are comparing your current rate with your prospect's new rate. Be patient for a better chance of success.

- ** Use Xdates to make your prospect feel a sense of urgency.

2. Smart activities are activities done by the right person.

- ** Who in your agency has more at stake than you, the agency owner? That doesn't mean you have to make all the calls and give all the quotes, but you should do and make the important calls and quotes.

- ** Delegate the less important calls to staff.

3. Smart activities are activities done for the right prospects.

- ** Don't waste time with prospects that don't recognize the value of having the right coverage with the right agency.

- ** Take the time to find clients/prospects that know the difference between price and cost.

4. Smart activities are activities delivered with the best message.

- ** Constantly look for ways to make your agency different.

- ** Give your clients/prospects reasons to do business with your agency. Sincerely tell your story and give and keep your promises.

- ** Give your prospects more than price to make a buying decision.

5. Smart activities are activities that may need persistence.

- ** Follow up! Follow up! Follow up! Follow up!

Conclusion

So, how do you make regular activities smart activities? The only way I know is to keep track of your results. How many calls did I make at what time to get how many people to answer? What did I say to the people who answered to get what result? How many? What result? Over and over. The secret to smart activity is knowing what works, and just as important, what doesn't work. No matter what the activity, keeping track of the results will make that activity more productive.

Good Luck . . .

Bill Lynch

 # Xdates

In 1974, Xdating was the most important activity a new or prospective agent could do. Important because Xdates were the foundation upon which agents built their agencies. Success was possible if you had and worked your Xdates. Without Xdates, your chance of success was greatly reduced.

So why was and still is Xdating important? When you Xdate, you almost magically convert a cold call from a cold prospect to a warm Xdate. Think about it. The Xdate has just told you when his policy expires. The Xdate by default permits you to call when his policy expires. If you asked the right questions, he told you about the cars he insures, the drivers who drive them, and who currently insures them. Most importantly, you are starting to build a relationship.

The reason I think it's possible to change a cold call into a warm Xdate is the lack of pressure you put on the prospect soon-to-be Xdate. You are not asking him to buy. You are not trying to give him a quote. All you are asking is what month his policies renew. No pressure! Also, you are asking to compare his coverage at some time in the future. But not now! I think the "not now" is the biggest reason Xdating works. Here are the words that worked for me. *My name is Bill Lynch with Farmers Insurance. I'd like to give you a quote on your auto/home insurance when your policy renews. What month does your policy renew?* Simple! You may have to help him pick a month, but even if it's the wrong month, that's OK. Eventually, with follow-up, you will have the opportunity to tell your story, share your promises, and, of course, compare coverage.

As a new agent, I spent most of my time Xdating. Xdates guaranteed I would have someone to talk to next month . . . and the month after that . . . and the month after that. I could almost predict how much success I'd have each month by the number of Xdates I had for that month. Xdates filled my pipeline.

To say Xdating was anything but boring would be a lie. To reduce the boredom, I played games with myself. I kept track of how many times I dialed the phone. (Yes, I said "dialed.") How many people answered? How many people hung up? How many people weren't very nice? The most important number I tracked was the number of wins I had. My wins were Xdates. Keeping track of my numbers helped me improve my results. My results were better when I called at the right time. My results were better when I smiled as I dialed the phone. My results were better when I was on a roll. Keeping track of my numbers not only helped avoid boredom but improved my results. My goal was to improve my results constantly.

I think Xdates are effective for at least three reasons.

1. By the time you give your presentation, you have had many opportunities to improve your relationship . . . The original call for the Xdate . . . The follow-up thank-you . . . At least, one, maybe more, contacts to see if your Xdate has

his renewal. You may even ask the "On a scale of one to ten, how would you rate your present agent?" question. For sure, you won't give your quote before you tell your story and share your promises. Then, of course, you will attempt to educate your Xdate about the importance of having the right coverage. Plenty of opportunities to build a relationship.

2. The Xdate makes your potential client feel a sense of urgency. His renewal date is approaching, and he knows he has to make a decision. No matter what decision he makes, you are still in the game. If he says yes, you now have a new client. If he says no, you still have an Xdate. Maintain your relationship and try again in a few months.

3. If you are patient and wait for your Xdate to receive his renewal, you can take advantage of comparing your current rate with his new rate. His insurance company, like yours, has rate increases. You may find him receptive because he is frustrated with his new rate. Even if your rate is still higher, his frustration may make him more willing to change because of the value you offer with your story and promises.

When I started, I got Xdates from the phone book, cold call lists, and cross directories. I had very few clients, and I did most of the calling myself. As my agency grew and I got busier, I hired Xdaters. A growing agency also gave me another source of Xdates. Current clients had cars, homes, boats, and businesses that we still didn't insure. I tried hard to make it clear to my new clients that we expected to insure all of their risks. We told them it made no sense to have more than one agent. We wanted to make sure there weren't gaps or overlaps in their coverage. We wanted to make sure they had all the available discounts. To do this, we needed to be their only insurance agent. This meant I had to have all of their Xdates.

Easier said than done. If your goal is getting Xdates, you have to find a way to stay focused. I stayed focused on my goals by keeping accurate records of my results. For instance, if my agency's goal is to find ten Xdates a day, it wouldn't make any difference how or who got them. Some of them could come from a part-time Xdater working a cold-call Internet list, some more might come from a CSR serving our current clients and I may find one or two while I'm doing a policy review. Surely a couple might be found marketing commercial business. It doesn't make any difference how or where we find our Xdates. The important thing is we get at least ten Xdates a day. Note that ten Xdates a day works out to fifty Xdates a week, two hundred a month, and in six short months, you have twelve hundred Xdates.

Staying focused meant at our weekly staff meeting we discussed our results. Were we ahead or behind schedule? What would we have to do to catch up? Keeping records helped us stay focused. We rarely were on target to meet our goal of ten Xdates a day. But that's OK! The fact that we were recording our weekly results almost guaranteed our results would be better than if we didn't keep track at all.

Conclusion

Whether you are a new or a seasoned agent, the Xdates you accumulate will be the foundation of your agency. Look at your agency. What do you do to market your agency? How does your agency grow? Are you happy with your agency's results? Will what you're doing get you to where you want to go? If not, re-examine what you do to attract new clients. If Xdating is not already a big part of your current plans, seriously consider Xdates as a way to grow your agency. Set your Xdate goals and stay focused on your goals.

Bill Lynch 503.407.7883 Bill@SimplifyAgencyGrowth.com

Do you use Xdate to grow YOUR business?

Do you quote prospects that haven't received their renewal? WHY?

CPSIA information can be obtained
at www.ICGtesting.com
Printed in the USA
FSHW02n1035090918
52079FS